ANDRE'S MOTHER

AND OTHER SHORT PLAYS

BY TERRENCE McNALLY

★

★

DRAMATISTS
PLAY SERVICE
INC.

2

TABLE OF CONTENTS

HIDDEN AGENDAS

CHARACTERS

CHAIRMAN
SUBSCRIBER LEADER
THEATER SUBSCRIBER
REPERTORY THEATRE DIRECTOR
DIRECTOR OF *HEDDA GABLER*
RESIDENT PLAYWRIGHT
THEATER SUBSCRIBER'S WIFE
OPERA HOUSE DIRECTOR
MRS. HARRIDAN
SYMPHONY SUBSCRIBER
SYMPHONY DIRECTOR
GENERAL SUBSCRIBER
LAST SUBSCRIBER

SETTING

The board room of a performing arts complex in any city in America big enough to afford one. There is a large Mapplethorpe on the wall. The board's constituents include one Afro-American, one Asian-American, one Hispanic-American, no Native American, one homosexual and it doesn't matter how many women. The time is now.

HIDDEN AGENDAS

CHAIRMAN.   Our theatres are full. The opera house, the symphony hall, the repertory theatre, the ballet, even the underground garage. I think we can pat ourselves on the back. *(The constituents pat themselves on the back.)* This meeting is adjourned. *(The boardroom doors burst open. A band of dread disgruntled subscribers storm the boardroom.)*

SUBSCRIBER LEADER.   We demand to be heard!

CHAIRMAN.   Go right ahead. We exist to please our audiences. *(Aside.)* Attend Mrs. Pettiworth! *(One of the board members has fainted at the intrusion.)*

THEATRE SUBSCRIBER.   We demand plays that illumine the human condition and elevate the soul but without resorting to frontal nudity or too many four-letter words.

REPERTORY THEATRE DIRECTOR.   That's why we're doing *Hedda Gabler* again.

DIRECTOR OF HEDDA GABLER.   *(Bristling.)* What's wrong with frontal nudity?

RESIDENT PLAYWRIGHT.   Exactly how many four-letter words are too many?

THEATRE SUBSCRIBER.   Eleven. We have no problem with ten or under. The same with frontal nudity. A little goes a long, long way. Especially male nudity. I mean, I was with my wife when that guy popped out.

THEATRE SUBSCRIBER'S WIFE.   And we didn't care for that avant-garde ballet where the women had hairy legs and armpits. What was your point? The human body is divine. Hairy women are disgusting. Ask anyone. Stick to *Swan Lake*. People can never get enough *Swan Lake*.

OPERA HOUSE DIRECTOR.   Our production of *La Boheme* was 3.8 million dollars over budget! That's right, 3.8 million! No one can accuse the opera of not giving the public what it wants.

MRS. HARRIDAN.   I paid for it. I'm mad for Verdi.

OPERA HOUSE DIRECTOR.   It's people like our own Mrs. Harridan who keep the arts alive and well in this country. Who needs the N.E.A.? Next season we're mounting a new production of *Aida*. We're calling it *Harridan* in your honor. Here's a preview. *(Curtains part to reveal Placido Domingo, Luciano Pavarotti, and Jose Carreras who sing "Celeste Harridan.")*

MRS. HARRIDAN.   What can I say, boys? I'm touched. I'm truly touched. The ability of the arts to touch our lives will never cease to amaze me. And people wonder why I spend so much money on the arts! Here, take 2 billion dollars for a new *Rink Cycle*.

OPERA HOUSE DIRECTOR.   *Ring* Cycle.

MRS. HARRIDAN.   Whatever. Oops, I'm late for the Disabled Modern Dancers' Luncheon. *(She exits.)*

SYMPHONY DIRECTOR.   I'm happy to announce that thanks to our subscriber marketing, no music written after the four Sea Interludes from *Peter Grimes* or before the last six Mozart symphonies will be played for the next five seasons.

SYMPHONY SUBSCRIBER.   I love contemporary music.

SYMPHONY DIRECTOR.   Get real. No one loves contemporary music. If you insist on it, there's a Tower Records kittycorner to the concert hall.

SYMPHONY SUBSCRIBER.   I like live music.

SYMPHONY DIRECTOR.   It was live when they recorded it. Next crank question?

GENERAL SUBSCRIBER.   We wants stars! You promised us Horowitz. He died. You teased us with Baryshnikov. He retired. Then Tom Cruise was rumored for the new Irene Fornes play. He did *Top Gun 2* for 10 million bucks. Where does that leave me, the poor ticket holder? I don't want to go to a concert or a ballet or a play with just people in it.

CHAIRMAN.   Neither do we. Hear, hear. I move the board pass a unanimous resolution condemning Tom Cruise for his lack of commitment to live theatre.

ENTIRE BOARD.   Moved and passed. *(Ovation. The board members pat themselves on the back.)*

LAST SUBSCRIBER.   I want to talk about art.

CHAIRMAN.   I don't think this is the time or place but thank you for sharing that. Meeting adjourned. *(The board members begin to leave.)*

LAST SUBSCRIBER.   What brings us into your halls and theatres is the expectation that the miracle of communication will take place. That a piece of music will touch us. That a dancer's movement will create a meaning where there was only space. Than an aria will speak to even one of us out there in a darkened auditorium in a way that no else ever has. That a playwright's truth will be revealed to an entire audience by an actor — totally clothed or not — in four-letter words or twenty-letter ones — whatever that truth demands. Words, sounds, gestures, feelings, thoughts! The things that connect us and make us human. The hope for that connection! That's why we fill your theatres. *(Most of the board has exited the boardroom during this.)* I can't imagine my life without the arts. *(He is alone in the boardroom. He looks at the Mapplethorpe.)* Thank you for listening to me.

STREET TALK

STREET TALK was first produced by the Manhattan Theatre Club (Lynn Meadow, Artistic Director; Barry Grove, Managing Director), in New York City, on May 18, 1988, as part of an evening entitled Urban Blight. It was directed by John Tillinger and Richard Maltby, Jr. The cast was as follows:

EUBIE BLADES .... Laurence Fishburne
CHARITY JONES .... Nancy Giles

CHARACTERS

EUBIE BLADES
CHARITY JONES

STREET TALK

A man enters. His name is Eubie Blades. He is whistling or singing to himself. Loudly. Like he owns the place. He turns upstage from us and begins to relieve himself. All the while he continues to whistle or sing. The tune is a song like "Stormy Weather."* After a while, he turns and looks right at us.

EUBIE.   You're just lucky I'm not taking a dump! *(He turns away and resumes relieving himself and continues singing "Stormy Weather.")*

"Is he really peeing, Harold?" "How should I know, Margaret?" "Well I'm sorry, but I hate this!" "We all do, Margaret. Thank goodness it's only a sketch." *(Eubie has used two distinct voices for Harold and Margaret. The whole time he has kept his back to us and continued to relieve himself. Next, he shakes himself off before buttoning his fly.)*

"Harold!" "Close your eyes!" *(Eubie turns and walks to the stage apron.)* I want to talk to you about audience confrontation. Not you personally! I just happened to be looking at you when I said it. Asshole! I wish you could see the expression on this guy's face. Utter panic. He thought I meant him. Relax, buddy. You're safe in your seat. But you're not, lady. I've had my eyes on you since I came out here. What are you laughing at, mister? You're next. Does anybody have a comb I can borrow? I bet you have *something* in there madame. You're not even looking. Never mind! I found mine. That was a test. You failed. *(He takes out a comb.)*

Where was I? Oh yeah, theatre of confrontation. This is a subject I can really get into. See, I cut my theatrical teeth on the 60s. I mean, you couldn't go to a play without some actor talking right to you or coming off the stage and sitting in your lap or trying to get you up on stage with him. No

* See Special Note on Songs and Recordings on copyright page.

sir, if you were uptight about actor/audience confrontation, it wasn't safe to go to the theatre in the 60s. *(He sits on the stage apron. During the following he will remove his shoes and socks and clean his feet of toe jam.)*

I know one poor SOB who loved the theatre but who didn't see a single show between *Hair* and *Agnes of God*. He was so terrified of some actor looking right at him and talking to him. He missed a lot of good shows, poor guy. I see him back there in the 7th row. I guess he figures it's 1988, the 60s were a long time ago, what the hell! I mean, this is a nice, cozy, not-for-profit theatre, they gave us *Claptrap* for Christ's sake! Am I right? Is he wrong? Just when you thought it was safe to go back into a theatre, along comes *Urban Blight!* I'm kidding, I'm kidding! *(A woman enters. Her name is Charity Jones.)*

This is Charity Jones. I'll tell you three things about her. One, she lives in a welfare hotel that you pay for. She's very grateful. Two, she can't find a public school less than a borough away that's willing to take even one of her three children. It's your Board of Ed. Three, Charity has a lovely singing voice. A real high, crystal clear, makes-you-feel-good kind of voice. Only I don't think Charity feels like singing right now. *(Charity shakes her head and sits beside him on the stage apron. During the following she will look at the audience with unblinking eyes.)*

I'm telling these nice people about confrontational theatre. The old days. When actors would roam the aisles. When you went to the theatre at your own peril. Anything could happen. A play could be about Vietnam and they'd throw pig's blood at you! Or civil rights and somebody would try to sign you up to join a protest march or register voters down South! Or gay stuff and you'd see two men, buff naked, a-hugging and a-kissing like it was the most natural thing in the world. But then all of a sudden it stopped. The war ended, the audience decided they had had enough of civil rights and they didn't care who was kissing who as long as they stayed on the stage and kept their clothes on. Some people, cynics I guess you'd have to call them, will tell you that it wasn't the audience that changed but the people that wrote the plays. What are they called? Playwrights. Nice word. That these playwrights stopped believing that theatre could end a war or get people of different races to live like brothers or get anyone to be a whole lot less uptight about who is sleeping with who. That these playwrights decided somewhere along the line that plays ought to go back to being more playful. The audience was delighted at this turn in events: they'd had their guts in a knot every time they took their seat in a theatre for the better part of a decade. The producers said great and raised the price of tickets. "We promise no one's ever gonna sit in your lap again and ask what you did to end a war but that'll he $37.50." So far it's working out fine. The audience is happy, the playwrights are sort of happy. This place looks pretty full. I've got my tickets for *Phantom of the Opera* sometime in '92. God's in his Heaven. All's right with the world. *Still! (He sighs. Charity takes his hand.)*

Sometimes I think, what if I jumped off this stage and swiped that lady's purse and ran like hell? I bet there's more money in there than I'll see in a year. What if I followed you home, yeah, *you!* and stood outside your door until you looked at me, really looked at me, and did something about the way I live? What if I took this knife I carry and plunged it into your heart, so maybe then you would know how much hate I carry in mine? What if some playwright could put me up here, the real me, so you would have some idea of how diminished my possibilities are? What if some actor could portray what it feels like not to eat maybe more than once every three days and then only what you wouldn't feed your animals? But you know all this. Theatre can't do it, brother. Yes, it can. Yes, it can. It doesn't want to. It's stopped trying. Who's kidding who? I'll be right outside when you leave here. I'll be holding an empty paper coffee cup. I'll be grateful for anything you can put in. Come on, Charity. *(They get up.)*

I just thought of one more "what if." What if Charity Jones felt like singing again? That would be one happy ending. *(They go. Black out.)*

PROPERTY LIST

Comb (EUBIE)

THE WIBBLY, WOBBLY, WIGGLY DANCE THAT CLEOPATTERER DID

THE WIBBLY, WOBBLY, WIGGLY DANCE THAT CLEOPATTERER DID

Tim and Tom are in bed. They have just made love.

TIM.   So, what do you think of women?

TOM.   *(After a very long pause.)* I like Madonna. I mean, she's very interesting. Politically. You know, as a symbol. She's got a great body.

TIM.   That wasn't quite my question.

TOM.   You mean, do I like them? Is that what you're asking?

TIM.   Yeah, I guess. You know, as people. As a sex.

TOM.   Sure I do. I like a lot of them a lot. Not all of them, of course. I don't like all men either. One of my best friends is a woman. We're very close. I tell her everything. I love her. I told her, "I'd marry you if you had a dick." I didn't say it quite like that, I mean, I'm not that gross, but it's true, if she were a man I'd marry her. If more women had dicks, I think there would be a real decline in homosexuality.

TIM.   You have a great chest. Really, really, really nice tits.

TOM.   Thank you. So do you. Think about it. I'm right. Women are so much more emotionally available than men. I mean, they're just *there*. Most men are somewhere else. Too much attitude. Too much macho my-dick-is-bigger-than-your-dick posturing if you ask me.

TIM.   My dick is bigger than your dick.

TOM.   So? I know. That doesn't threaten me. Big deal.

TIM.   It is, as a matter of fact.

TOM. That's just what I'm talking about. A woman would never make a remark like that.

TIM. Jesus, I would hope not!

TOM. I'm being serious. You asked me what I thought was a serious question and I'm trying to give you a serious answer.

TIM. I'm sorry, but what did you say your name was? Jim, right?

TOM. Tom. You're Tim, I'm Tom.

TIM. Tim-Tom. Cute. We sound like twins! Are you gonna want to cum again?

TOM. I don't know. We just did. Jesus! I know most men have a problem with intimacy but you seem to have a problem with transitions. Women, your big dick, child actors, do you want to cum again? — all in 30 seconds.

TIM. I cut to the chase. I asked you what you thought about women. You told me — not much. So then I asked you if you want to cum again. I assume you're saying no.

TOM. I said, I don't know. And I think a lot of women! I don't know where you got nothing from.

TIM. I didn't say nothing. I said not much. *(He gets out of bed.)* I think, my friend, that what I shall do is this: I shall bid you a fond farewell.

TOM. I thought you were going to stay over. I mean, I thought we had discussed that. Settled it.

TIM. I have a big day tomorrow. I could use a good sleep. I don't usually sleep well in strange beds. And then there's the problem of sharing the bathroom with a stranger. You know, the smells. My mother used to tell me, "Light a match." There ain't enough matches on this planet for when I'm done in there. Believe me, you'll thank me for this in the morning. *(He starts dressing.)*

TOM. I'd like you to stay.

TIM. I better not. It's like I said: sleep, the bathroom, etc. etc. Besides, if we're not going to get it on again, what'd be the point? Oh, shit!

TOM. What's the matter?

TIM. Is tomorrow the 4th?

TOM.   Yeah, I think so.

TIM.   It's my girlfriend's birthday. I want to get her something really nice this year. Something from Tiffany's. You think Tiffany's has anything for under a hundred bucks?

TOM.   Sure. Key rings, and ... hmm ... what else?

TIM.   You can't give a woman a key ring for her birthday. That's like giving her a baseball bat or a football. Pam would take one look at a key ring and say "Thank you, Tim" but her heart would break in two. I respect her too much to give her a fucking key ring. Do they have something feminine for under a hundred bucks?

TOM.   Those are my shorts.

TIM.   Yeah?

TOM.   They are if they're Calvin Klein.

TIM.   There's another brand??!! *(He comes over to Tom who pulls down the waistband and reads the label.)*   I think that Marky Mark is a queer. You telling me a straight man would pose for an ad like that? Pam thinks he's a queer, too. Women have an infallible instinct when it comes to that. They can spot one a mile away.

TOM.   They're mine.

TIM.   Sorry. *(He changes shorts.)* I want to get a ripped body like Marky Mark's. I know I've got a better voice but it's not enough anymore. They all want ripped bodies, too. That fucking gym. I've spent a fucking fortune there. You know, you should work out more. I mean, you've got a nice body, don't get me wrong, it's very nice, but it's not exactly ripped. Ripped is in. Men and women. Straight and gay. Look at Madonna, ripped to hell. Can you imagine the kid she and Marky Mark could produce?

TOM.   I think those are my socks.

TIM.   Sorry. I don't want you to think I'm ripping you off. I'm not into that. A lot of guys, they come over, they give the guy a hand job and then they're out of there. I'm not like that. I'm more tender-er. Is that a word?

TOM.   Without the qualifying adjective, it is.

TIM.   I'm more tender. Yeah, you're right. That sounds better. Anyway, I respect the feminine side of my nature. I recognize it, which is more than most men do. That's why I get repeats. Most guys in my line don't get repeats. There's no reason to be nice. To be tender. They're not gonna see the guy again and they both know it. Face it, most men, when they've cum, you're out of there. They're off on cloud 9 thinking about what they're gonna tell their wife.

TOM.   I don't have a wife. I'm gay.

TIM.   I said most men.

TOM.   I'm really, really gay and I'd like you to stay. I'm lonely.

TIM.   I'm sorry to hear that. *(He sits on edge of the bed and puts his hand on Tom's face.)* You know what you need? A lover.

TOM.   I had a lover.

TIM.   Or a girlfriend.

TOM.   I don't want a girlfriend.

TIM.   How do you know?

TOM.   I have a girlfriend.

TIM.   They're better for some things, girls are. Women are.

TOM.   Not what I want.

TIM.   What's that?

TOM.   I don't know.

TIM.   Not this?

TOM.   Of course not this.

TIM.   Women are good for more than this.

TOM.   People are good for more than this.

TIM.   Some people.

TOM.   What's so wrong with this, all of a sudden?

TIM.   Nothing. I didn't say that.

TOM.   I had a good time.

TIM.   It was mutual.

TOM.   So let's not analyze it.

TIM.   It just wasn't enough.

TOM.   I know that.

TIM.   Do you fuck what's-her-name?

TOM.   None of your business. No. Yes. Once.

TIM.   Did you like it?

TOM.   Obviously I liked it or I wouldn't have done it.

24

TIM.   You'd be surprised how many straight men don't.

TOM.   You'd be surprised how many gay men don't. But just as obviously I didn't like it enough or I would have done it again.

TIM.   Does what's-her-big name have big tits?

TOM.   As a matter of fact, she does.

TIM.   I love big-titted women. Pam has tiny tits, practically non-existent, but what the hell, she's got a big heart and she thinks the sun rises and sets out of my asshole, and you can't have everything, right? Did you go down on what's-her-name?

TOM.   No! And I wish you'd stop calling her that. Her name is Janet.

TIM.   Janet! That's a name you don't hear much anymore. I love eating out a woman. I hate it when guys call it "Hair Pie." It's such a gross expression for such a beautiful thing. Maybe the next time you fuck Janet, you'll try it.

TOM.   Can we change the subject?

TIM.   Okay, you don't want to talk about women? We won't talk about women.

TOM.   We're not talking about women. I don't know what we're talking about but we're not talking about women.

TIM.   You need someone to shoot the shit with. We all do. That and our space. We all need our space. Pam gave me a great T-shirt that said it all. "I want you to: Fuck me, beat me, shit on me, tell me you love me and then get the hell out of here." I loved that shirt. It got ruined in the laundromat. All the letters ran. When we get married, one of the first things I'm gonna buy us is our own washer-dryer. The ones in commercial laundromats are just too violent for nicer things, you know?

TOM.   This conversation is making me so sad.

TIM.   It's not me?

TOM.   No. You asked me what I thought about women and now you're telling me what's wrong about men!

TIM.   There's nothing wrong with men or women. They're just different. You're a nice man. I can tell that. (*He pulls the covers back. Tom is naked now.*)

TOM.   Why did you do that?

TIM.   I just wanted to look at you. You watched me while I got dressed. Fair's fair. You've got a great dick.

TOM.   Thank you.

TIM.   Men are so funny about really looking at each other's dicks. We're too shy with each other. Pam studies my dick for hours. She says she's got it memorized. Every vein, every contour. I hate my dick. I think it's ugly. Yours is much nicer. I'd trade in a flash. Goodbye, sweet dick, and choirs of angels sing thee to thy rest. (*He pulls the cover back up over Tom.*) One of these days, it's going to make the right person very, very happy.

TOM.   What? You do fortune tellings on the side?

TIM.   Go ahead, make light. I'm trying to tell you something serious.

TOM.   You mean, Mr. Right, One Day My Prince Will Come, Keanu Reeves?

TIM.   Well, maybe not Keanu Reeves. He's a movie star. Get real.

TOM.   You mean, lower my expectations?

TIM.   You're just looking for love in all the wrong places. (*He gives him a kiss on the cheek and stands up.*) So. All good things must come to an end.

TOM.   Oh, your ... the money. It's ... (*He takes the money from where he had hidden it.*) Now I'm really embarrassed. But listen, you could have been an axe murderer or a maniac. You never know what you're getting into when you meet someone. I had a friend who jumped out his window and broke both his knees, he got so frightened by someone he brought home with him. The guy took everything. The TV, the stereo, his computer. His father's ring even and his father had been dead only about six weeks. And Mark's lying four floors below at the bottom of an airshaft. This way you could have murdered me but you wouldn't have found the money.

TIM.   I would never have murdered you. I would never murder anyone.

TOM.   I know. Here. (*He gives Tim the money.*)

TIM.   Thank you. (*He begins counting it.*) It's not that I don't trust you. It's just better this way. No misunderstanding. You know, I get to your elevator and the $100 has mysteriously shrunk to an 80. Then I get pissed off and start banging on your door and — not that I'm saying you're the sort who would deliberately do such a thing. But like I said, it's just better this way. One hundred dollars. Slam, bam, thank you ma'am. That was a bad joke, I'm sorry. I'm not a crude person. I wish you well in your pursuit of love. I wish us both well. This is always the hard part: saying goodbye. I'd like to give you the biggest kiss and hug anybody ever had but that would mean I cared for you and I don't and you don't care for me and the truth is we'll never see each other again! I lied to you. I don't have repeats. There are no repeats in this business. *C'est la vie. C'est la guerre. C'est la* everything. I hate the look your doorman is going to give me.

TOM.   Why did you ask me what I thought about women?

TIM.   It was a trick question: I was curious what you thought about men.

TOM.   And I failed. "Not much" was your verdict.

TIM.   I think we all fail one another a lot lately. Male, female; straight, gay.

TOM.   A pretentious hustler, just my luck.

TIM.   A lonely faggot, so what else is new?

TOM.   I'm sorry. I didn't mean that.

TIM.   Neither did I.

TOM.   You're right, this is the worse part.

TIM.   I'll let myself out. Call me sometime. I left my card on your table.

TOM.   I will. For sure. I'd like that. *(They shake hands.)*

TIM.   Me, too. Goodnight.

TOM.   Goodbye. *BREAKFAST AT TIFFANY'S!* You saw the movie, now live it.

TIM.   Everytime I buy her sexy lingerie, I get excited and I rip it off. I don't think something from Tiffany's is going to turn me on. *Ciao, bello. (Tim goes. Tom looks at the card and begins to rip it up into a million little pieces.)*

THE END

PROPERTY LIST

1 pair of Calvin Klein man's underpants (TIM)
One hundred dollars in loose bills (TOM)
Business card (TOM)

PRELUDE
& LIEBESTOD

CHARACTERS

CONDUCTOR — Mid-40s, handsome, magnetic, moves magnificently.

CONDUCTOR'S WIFE — Mid-to-late 30s, beautiful, perfectly groomed, elegant carriage and gestures.

MAN — Mid-to-late 20s, informally dressed, not as sure of himself as he'd like to be or thinks he is.

CONCERTMASTER — Mid-50s, rough looks, florid complexion, looks and acts as if he's seen it all. He has.

SOPRANO — Early 30s. Full-figured. Still very green on the concert platform but she doesn't know it.

TIME

The present

SETTING

The stage of a concert hall

PRELUDE
& LIEBESTOD

Lights come up on a conductor's podium, a small, square raised platform about 15 inches high. There is a waist-high railing running the length of the upstage side of it.

Sounds of a symphony orchestra tuning up at random.

Spot up on a beautiful woman in a box seat somewhat upstage of the podium. She is the Conductor's Wife. She is perfectly dressed. She looks at her program. She looks at her watch. She looks at the orchestra in the orchestra level below her. She looks up at the higher tiers and balcony above her.

Spot up on a Man in an orchestra level seat stage left, also somewhat upstage of the Conductor's podium. He is looking at the Conductor's Wife through a pair of opera glasses. She is not aware of this.

Spot up on the Concertmaster who is seated in a chair just a little downstage right of the podium. He raps with his bow on his violin stand and gives the note.

An unseen symphony orchestra tunes up.

The Conductor's Wife opens her purse and takes out a small box of mints.

The Man continues to stare at her through the opera glasses. At the same time, he reaches in his breast pocket and takes out a roll of Lifesavers.

The house lights dim in the concert hall where the Conductor's Wife and Man are sitting.

At the same time, the lights will come up on the concert stage, i.e. the theatre itself.

A spotlight hits a door leading to the backstage area. After a longer time than necessary, it is opened by unseen hands and the Soprano enters to strong applause. She is in full regalia.

As Soprano moves towards podium, she smiles at the unseen orchestra. The Concertmaster taps his bow on his stand in approval.

Soprano turns her back to orchestra (and us, in doing so) and bows deeply to heavy applause.

Now Soprano makes a great deal of arranging the panels of her dress and stole as the Concertmaster finally sits in a chair just left and a little downstage of the podium. Her back will be to us but we will see her in profile as she turns from time to time to take a sip of water from a glass on a low table next to her chair or turns to the other side to smile at the Concertmaster.

Silence.

The spotlight has gone again to the door leading to the backstage area. It waits there. Again the door is opened by unseen hands. No one appears.

Silence in the auditorium. Someone coughs. Someone else shushes them. Door starts to swing shut, then is swiftly pulled wide open as Conductor hurries through.

Tumultuous applause.

Conductor moves swiftly to podium and bows deeply. The Man has risen and is clapping wildly.

MAN.   Bravo! Bravo! *(Conductor's Wife is applauding. Conductor leaps off podium and goes to Concertmaster and shakes his hand vigorously. Ovation continues as Conductor crosses to Soprano and kisses her hand, then cheek. Man continues to stand and applaud.)*

Bravo! Bravo! *(Conductor's Wife has stopped applauding. Conductor has returned to podium for final bow to audience [which means his back is to us] as applause begins to diminish. Man continues to stand and applaud. This time his voice is especially prominent as the general ovation continues to subside.)*

Bravo! Bravo! *(Conductor looks to Man. Eye contact is made. Conductor's Wife looks at Man. Conductor looks up at Wife and smiles, then turns his back to concert hall audience and faces orchestra [us]. Conductor is delighted with his reception. He gives orchestra members a self-deprecating grin and raised eyebrows. Silence. He gets serious. He passes his hands over his face. He takes a deep breath. Man shatters the silence.)*

We love you! *(Conductor ignores this. Angry shushes from audience. Conductor reaches to music stand in front of him and closes the score. Gasps and whispers from the audience. He picks up baton. He raises both arms. He waits. He throws the baton onto the music stand and raises both arms again but this time gives the downbeat almost at once. Wagner's Prelude to* Tristand und Isolde *is off and running.)*
CONDUCTOR.   *(After the fourth rest.)* I love these pauses.... Come on you suckers, play for me. Play through me, music. Course through me. Surge. Fill me. I am you. This is it.... God, that was good. Now we're off and running. I'm up here already. That was quick. I like it up here. The view is glorious. Fill, lungs. Heave, bosom. Burst, heart. *(At this point, the*

sound of the orchestra is considerably diminished and the Conductor will seem to be speaking from within his own private place. The music will be more of a "surround" than a presence.)

There were no empty seats. Clean as a whistle. There's no one better than me. Is there? No one even close. God, I love Wagner. That one in the fifth row. I've seen him. Where? In your dreams, asshole. We don't do that anymore You wanna bet? Oh shut up! Hey, third cello, look at me! Yes, you! Where did they find you? Yes, you're too loud. You think I'd be looking at you like this if you weren't? Jesus, where was I? Sometimes I think I do this on automatic. There we are, right on target! Somebody up there likes me. Yeah, Wagner, asshole. The Big Kraut in das Himmel Himself. I feel his eyes burning right into my back. He's mentally undressing me. They all are. All 2,187 of them plus the 131 in standing room. Maybe I could steal a look. Are you crazy? She's right up there in a box. She's always right up there in a box. I d like to see her in a box. It's her box I'm sick of. You don't mean that. I don't mean that. You love her. I love you. *(He looks over his shoulder to Wife who is reading something in her program.)*

She's reading! The fucking bitch is reading and you're conducting your fucking ass off. Fuck that shit. Bitch. You wanted to be married. No, you wanted to have children. You have to be married to have children. No, you have to be married to have children if you want to be the principal conductor of a big symphony orchestra with a big stuffy endowment. You're pissed off because you've got the hots for some groupie in the fifth row and you're goddamn wife is right up there watching every move you make. Eagle eyes. Bionic ears. She can see and hear through lead walls if I'm talking to another man. It's one thing to be straight; it's another to be in a straight jacket. *(Suddenly aware of the Concertmaster.)*

What are you looking at, asshole? I swear to God, sometimes I think he's calling me an asshole under his breath through the whole concert.

CONCERTMASTER. Asshole.

CONDUCTOR. There! Right now! I'm positive he's doing

it. I'd like to see him get up here and conduct, he thinks he's so great. They probably all think they can conduct better than me. Sorry to disillusion you, assholes! That's why I'm up here and you're down there. Whoever said it was right: it is lonely at the top. It's lonely anywhere.

MAN.   Look at me. You know I'm here.

WIFE.   *(Still looking at program.)* Now that is what I call a stunning outfit. Oscar De La Renta. I should have guessed.

CONCERTMASTER.   Asshole.

SOPRANO.   Fuck you, too!

CONCERTMASTER.   I wasn't talking to you.

SOPRANO.   What did I do to him? I'm sorry, but we can't all be Kirsten Fucking Flagstad.

MAN.   Turn around. You know you want to.

CONDUCTOR.   He's talking to you. Go ahead. This climax. It's a perfect place. Shit! I can't. You blew it, asshole.

MAN.   You know what I'd do if I had you alone with me? I have it all planned. I'd undress you. With my teeth. I'd start with a button. This button. *(He touches his collar button.)* Pop!

WIFE.   Oh God, I hope Ralph can get away for that weekend when he's conducting in London. I don't think I can stand another week without him. I wonder what he'd do if he knew. Kill me. Punish me through the children. Both.

CONDUCTOR.   Turn, turn, turn. To everything there is a season. The Beatles? The Turtles. Ten minutes with someone like that. Less. It doesn't take long. I want you so bad, fifth row.

CONCERTMASTER.   Bloody, bleeding, blooming asshole.

CONDUCTOR.   If I had a face like yours I'd kill myself.

SOPRANO.   It's nearly me. There's got to be better ways to earn a living.

CONDUCTOR.   Why did you have to be out there tonight, fatal beauty, or why did you have to be up there, faithful adoring wife? Why couldn't tonight be next week in London? I'm doing the Mahler *9th.* I'm always so drained after the Mahler *9th.* Drained and horny.

MAN.   Look at me. They say if you stare at someone's left

earlobe long enough, eventually it begins to burn a hole and they turn around.

CONDUCTOR. It's all in the music. The longing, the learning. The impossibility. I am loved. I want to love. I've never found anyone as interesting as me. As lovable. As worthy of my undivided attention. Fifth row is one thing, her up there is another. I'm talking about a whole other kettle of fish. *(The Prelude is drawing to an end. The Soprano stands and makes ready to sing.)* Good God, it's her turn already. Come on, cow, sing it, swing it, shake it, bend it.

MAN. Maybe it's the right earlobe. *(Soprano begins to sing. At first the music will be at concert hall volume, then subside to the level of the Prelude. Although her back is to us throughout, it should be clear that the Soprano is deeply involved with singing and communicating with her audience out front.)*

CONCERTMASTER. You're flat. Get up there, get up there!

WIFE. Now that's a gorgeous voice.

MAN. Sharp as ever.

CONDUCTOR. You're singing through the wrong hole, honey. This is twat music. Listen to it. Listen to the words. God, if I had your instrument!

SOPRANO. Place the tone properly. Support it. Always legato. Thatta girl.

WIFE. If I could sing like that!

MAN. They like her! They actually like her!

CONCERTMASTER. That's more like it. *(Surtitles will appear throughout.)*

SURTITLE.
"Mild und leise wie er lächelt,
wie das Auge hold er öffnet,
seht ihr's, Freunde? Seht ihr's nicht?
Immer lichter, wie er leuchtet,
stern-umstrahlet hoch sich hebt?
Seht ihr's nicht?

CONDUCTOR. Do you know that the words mean? Sing it like you know what it meant. It's about love. It's about dying. It's about trans-fan-fucking-figuration. Sing it like you meant it.

SURTITLE.
"Wie das Herz ihm mutig schwillt,
voll und hehr im Busen ihm quillt?
Wie den Lippen, wonnig mild,
süsser Atem sanft entweht,
Freunde! Seht! Fühlt und seht ihr's nicht?
CONDUCTOR.   This is not enough. Conducting it is not
enough. Singing it is not enough. Writing it is not enough.
Experience it. Love-death. Love-death. *Liebestod.*
CONCERTMASTER.   What is he doing?
CONDUCTOR.   You're behind, honey, catch up, catch up!
SOPRANO.   This is not the tempo we agreed —!
WIFE.   That man looks like Ralph.
MAN.   He's losing you, lady.
CONDUCTOR.   Who do you love the most? Who do you
love the best?
SURTITLE.
"Höre ich nur diese Weise
die so wundervoll und leise,
Wonne klagend, alles sagend,
mild versöhnend aus ihm tönend,
in mich dringet, auf sich schwinget,
hold erhallend um mich klinget?
Heller schallend, mich umwallend,
sind es Wellen sanfter Lüfte?
Sind es Wogen wonniger Düfte?
CONDUCTOR.   What is transfiguration but an orgasm
coupled with a heart attack?
SURTITLE.
"Wie sie schwellen, mich umrauschen,
soll ich atmen, soll ich lauschen?
Soll ich schlurfen, untertauchen?
Süss in Düften mich verhauchen?
CONDUCTOR.   Wagner knew a lot about fucking. I bet
that guy in the fifth row does, too. My wife knows nothing
about fucking. I'd like to fuck the entire world. No, I'd like
to fuck every attractive man, woman and child in the world.
Child over 11. No, 14. 15, 15. Fuck it.

SURTITLE.
"In dem wogenden Schwall, in dem tönenden Schall,
in des Welt-Atems wehendem All
ertrinken, versinken —,
unbewusst, höchste Lust —.
CONDUCTOR.   It's over already. Shit. I don't even remember it beginning. *(Long pause as music fades to silence.)*
WIFE.   Oh shit, now the Bruckner *4th.*
CONCERTMASTER.   Oh shit, now the Bruckner *4th.*
SOPRANO.   Isn't anybody going to clap?
MAN.   Now he's got to turn around. *(Ovation begins. A tremendous one. Conductor doesn't move. Instead, he remains with his back to concert hall audience. Soprano accepts ovation with great humility. Above all the others.)* We love you! *(Conductor picks up baton and raps with it.)*
CONDUCTOR.   Again! From the top!
CONCERTMASTER.   But —! *(Conductor gives downbeat. Soprano looks startled but takes her seat. Man sits. Wife remains standing in her box, looking concerned, but will eventually sit. The* Tristan *Prelude will seem very loud at first. It will finally settle at same level of volume as previous rendition of it.)*
CONDUCTOR.   Give them profile. Feed it to them. They love your profile. Move the body. They come for body movement. Those fabulous, famous, far-reaching shoulders. Magnificent arms on a mighty torso. High flying adored. You and Evita! Wiggle your ass. Tight firm buttocks worthy of someone half your age. Make them think about your cock and balls. Are they large? Is he clipped? Is he good? I'm terrific, baby. Ask her. Ask him. Ask anyone who's had the pleasure of my acquaintance. It's them who don't measure up. It's them who fail me. They're fucking me. Taking. Drawing my strength. Where's my equal? My match? I'm so alone. Up here. Everywhere. I really love this pause. What is this music really about? What is anything really about? I don't think this is such a great theme. I've written better but he's Richard Wagner — big fucking deal — and I am Marie of Rumania — big fucking deal. This music always makes me think of certain kinds of sex. Hot late afternoon damp sheets sweaty

38

grunting people outside blinds drawn dark dirty make it last as long as you can come crazy, scream, rip the sheets, howl like a Werewolf, hurt him, hurt her, ouchy kind of sex. This will be in all the papers tomorrow. For 24 hours I'll be the most famous person in the world. 48 maybe. 72. Then next week when the magazines come out there will be a new spurt of fame. Then a gradual subsiding until the first major memorial service. A plaque will go up somewhere. Probably outside the hall. God knows, no one ever, anywhere, ever again will listen to this music without thinking of me. *(He glances at Wife. Their eyes meet and hold.)*

You had the most beautiful skin and breasts and throat and everything when we met. They weren't enough. Nothing has ever been enough. The children. They're not real. Real in themselves but not real to me. Not real enough. Nothing, no one is real enough. I am the only person in the world and I cannot bear the pain of being so alone. I'm only alive when I come — the way I want to be alive — ecstatic, half-conscious, eyes closed, brain flaring, words, thoughts inadequate. *(He glances at the Man.)*

The only satisfying sexual experience I ever had was with a man.

MAN.   Finally.

CONDUCTOR.   The kind of sexual experience this music is about.

CONCERTMASTER.   This is more like it.

WIFE.   Go on.

SOPRANO.   I hate it when they look at me.

CONDUCTOR.   I was 22 years old, studying in Milan, already made my debut in Salzburg that summer, an instant sensation, the old fool got sick, I took over, the Bruckner *4th* and the *Pathetique*.... God, that would have been next on the program, I loathe Bruckner! Who couldn't conduct the *Pathetique?* The toast of Europe. God, I was handsome that year. I could spend hours in front of the mirror talking to myself. I'd make faces. Scowl, smile. Flirt with myself. I could even get myself hard. This bastard ... what was his name? ... he was a journalist, political ... the apartment was near the

Piazzo della Republica ... it was over a pharmacy ... the steps
were exhausting ... deep, steep Renaissance steps ... there was
a terra cotta Madonna in the apartment ... he said it was a
Lucca della Robbia and I wanted to believe him ... God, I
was already so famous but I was still so easily impressed! ...
what the fuck was your name?

MAN.   Giorgio, Piero, Giacomo, Giuseppe, Gaetano.

WIFE.   Does it matter?

CONCERTMASTER.   Asshole!

MAN.   Carlo, Mario, Fausto, Arturo, Vittorio, Fred.

CONDUCTOR.   Guglielmo! Guglielmo Tell. Kidding, kidding. No, I'm not. Guglielmo Bianchini. He knew who I was.
He must have. Everyone did. My picture was everywhere that
summer. I was so beautiful that year — I was perfect — I was
all I wanted — all anyone could ever possibly want — and
this cocksucker, this arrogant wop, this goddamn glorious
dago, he led me on and on and on. A touch, a glance, a
brush of thigh but no more. I wasn't even sure he was queer.
Weeks went on like this. Torture. No one knew why I was
staying in Milan. I'm doing research. What research? You
know everything. It's true. I did. About music. But the promise of this person kept me on.

WIFE.   My poor darling.

MAN.   After the concert, when I ask for your autograph, I
will pass you a slip of paper with my telephone number on
it. No name, just a number. You'll know what to do with it.

SOPRANO.   I better be paid twice for this. And I'm cer-
tainly not singing the TANNHAUSER for an encore.

CONCERTMASTER.   Asshole, asshole, asshole.

CONDUCTOR.   Finally, there was a weekend when his father, a widower and some sort of famous judge or lawyer,
would be out of town at their place in Como. I went to the
apartment. The door was ajar. There was no sign of him. I
wandered through the empty apartment. It had been a
palazzo. Everything was huge — molded, sculpted, ornate. I
went into a bedroom — it must have been the father's —
yes, that is where the Lucca Della Robbia was and I stood

looking at this enormous bed and then I felt — I feel! — hands on me from behind. I didn't turn around. Don't want to. *(The Soprano stands and begins to sing the* Liebestod *again. Only this time the surtitles will be in English.)*

Hands here, hands there. Hands over my eyes, hands over my mouth. Four hands. Someone else is there. I didn't struggle. My clothes are being taken off — were being taken off — I don't know what tense I'm in — what tense I want to be in — the past is too painful, the present too forlorn — and I am being stripped and stroked and I am blindfolded and I am led to the bed and my cock is so hard and I am put on the bed and I let myself be tied spread eagle to it — no one has ever done this to me and I do not resist — and when it is done I am left there for what seems like hours and my hard on will not subside and once even it threatens to explode and I pray to the unseen Della Robbia Madonna above me not to let me come and I know this is blasphemy and I know that she forgives and understands because she is a good mother — all mothers are good mothers — and oh, it is so — unimaginably intense to be there like that with him.

SOPRANO.
"How gently and quietly he smiles,
how fondly he opens his eyes!
See you, friends? Do you not see?
How he shines ever higher,
soaring on high, stars sparkling around him?
Do you not see?
How his heart proudly swells
and, brave and full, pulses in his breast?
How softly and gently from his lips
sweet breath flutters: —
see, friends! Do you not feel and see it?
Do I alone hear this melody
which, so wondrous and tender
in its blissful lament, all-revealing,
gently pardoning, sounding from him,

pierces me through, rises above,
blessedly echoing and ringing round me?"
CONDUCTOR.   And after a while I am unblindfolded and
see my captors — Guglielmo and a young woman who can
only be his twin sister; she is a feminine mirror image of him
— and they are both nude and more beautiful than anyone
I have ever seen — more beautiful than even I was that summer — and she straddles me and lowers herself on my cock
very slowly just once and I almost come but I pray and then
he — Guglielmo — what an absurd name! — put his mouth
on my cock and moves it up and down the length of it just
once and again I almost come and have to pray and then
they both just looked at me and I said, "Please, make me
come." *"Prego, farmi morire"* is what I said. "Please make me
die." I didn't know the Italian for "come," you see. *"Prego,
farmi morire."*
SOPRANO.
"Resounding yet more clearly, wafting about me,
are they waves of refreshing breezes?
Are they clouds of heavenly fragrance?
As they swell and roar round me,
shall I breathe them, shall I listen to them?"
CONDUCTOR.   And they just smiled at each other. He
kissed one of her breasts. She touched his cock. I knew they
weren't really twins. I wondered if they were even brother
and sister. She took her panties, pink, and ran them the
length of my body, toe to head. Then she very slowly pushed
them into my mouth, gagging me with them. I didn't resist.
The whole time our eyes held. He blindfolded me again. I
felt their hands on me, their mouths. Everywhere. And then
I heard the door close. After a while I stopped thinking
about the Madonna and praying to her and when I thought
of Guglielmo and Francesca — I'd named her by then, you
see; I have a great need to know the name of things — adoring me I couldn't hold back any longer. I didn't want to and
I came with an intensity that amazes me to this day and that
I have never since even remotely equalled. I could feel my
own semen on my lips, on my eyes, in my hair. Guglielmo

and Francesca.

MAN.   What are your secrets?

WIFE.   I only deceive him sexually.

CONCERTMASTER.   This is beautiful. I'll grant him that.

SOPRANO.

"Shall I sip them, plunge beneath them,

to expire in sweet perfume?"

CONDUCTOR.   Of course, after I came I lost all interest in the game and wanted to be free. More importantly, I lost all interest in them. I lay there feeling the flood of semen grow watery, then dry and caked on my stomach, chest and face. Hours passed. I could not free myself. The blindfold, the gag held firm. Once, I relaxed enough to mentally relive the episode and I immediately got hard and came again, though not nearly so much this time. The next thing I knew I heard a strange woman's scream, a man's angry voice and pretty soon I'm unblindfolded and the room is filled with people, most of whom are police, and an irate, bewildered couple in their 60s who had returned to their apartment after an outdoor performance of NABUCCO in the Piazza del Duomo and who was I, how did I get there, what was I doing? Translation: what had I done? I never saw Guglielmo or Francesca again. It wasn't their apartment, of course. Were they even real? The orgasm was.

SOPRANO.   "In the surging swell, in the ringing sound,

in the vast wave of the word's breath —

to drown, to sink

unconscious — supreme bliss!"

CONDUCTOR.   Once I asked her to tie me to the bed and sit on me. She loved it.

WIFE.   This is so beautiful.

CONDUCTOR.   Once I tied her. She loved it.

CONCERTMASTER.   I gotta hand it to you, asshole.

CONDUCTOR.   Once I let a fan — someone like you, sweetheart — try it but I'd had too much to drink or he'd had too much to drink or he smelled funny or he said something I didn't like — like Nixon wasn't such a bad President — or he was too big or too little or one of the ten million other things that don't let you connect perfectly with another person. That afternoon in Milan when I was young and first famous and still thought the answer to a good life was in my work, in other people, in success, seems so long ago. There is no other person. There is a woman in a box who is my wife and bore me two children. There is a man in the fifth row who entertains fantasies about someone who he thinks is me. There is a concertmaster who detests me but not half as much as I detest myself. There is a cow guest soprano who sings music that has no meaning for her in a perfectly ravishing voice. And so it goes. There are a lot of people. Five billion of us I read just this morning and pretty soon there will be six billion and the only time I ever felt connected to any of them was when I was 22-years-old and tied spread-eagled to a retired Milanese optometrist's bed wanting to be made love to by two people I'm not even sure exist. *(The last measures of the* Liebestod *are sounding. Conductor takes a small Japanese seppuku blade from the music stand in front of him.)*

I know why I'm doing this. Wagner knew. Tristan and Isolde knew. That's four of us. Fuck the rest. *(He plunges the blade into his abdomen. Blood spurts onto the music stand. Conductor's face is transfigured. Another standing ovation has begun. Soprano bows deeply to the audience in the concert hall. The Man is already on his feet.)*

MAN.   Bravo! We love you! *(Wife rises in her box, afraid. Conductor continues to stare straight ahead, blood spurting from him onto the music stand, the transfigured, ecstatic expression on his face. The ovation is mounting. The Concertmaster is busily gathering his music, ready to leave the stage.)*

CONCERTMASTER.   Asshole. *(Lights fade to black.)*

END OF PLAY

PROPERTY LIST

Concert program (CONDUCTOR'S WIFE)
Opera glasses (MAN)
Violin and bow (CONCERTMASTER)
Purse (CONDUCTOR'S WIFE) with:
    box of mints
Roll of Lifesavers candy (MAN)
Music stand (CONCERTMASTER)
Glass of water (SOPRANO)
Baton (CONDUCTOR)
Small Japanese seppuku blade (CONDUCTOR)

SOUND EFFECTS

Symphony orchestra tuning up
Applause

ANDRE'S MOTHER

A Sketch for *Urban Blight*

ANDRÉ'S MOTHER

A Sketch for *Urban Blight*

Four people enter. They are nicely dressed and carry white helium-filled balloons on a string.

They are Cal, a young man; Arthur, his father; Penny, his sister; and André's Mother.

CAL.   You know what's really terrible? I can't think of anything terrific to say. Goodbye. I love you. I'll miss you. And I'm supposed to be so great with words!

PENNY.   What's that over there?

ARTHUR.   Ask your brother.

CAL.   It's a theatre. An outdoor theatre. They do plays there in the summer. Shakespeare's plays. *(To Andre's Mother.)* God, how much he wanted to play Hamlet. It was his greatest dream. I think he would have sold his soul to play it. He would have gone to Timbuktu to have another go at that part. The summer he did it in Boston, he was so happy!

PENNY.   Cal, I don't think she...! It's not the time. Later.

ARTHUR.   You son was a ... the Jews have a word for it ...

PENNY.   *(Quietly appalled.)* Oh my God!

ARTHUR.   *Mensch,* I believe it is and I think I'm using it right. It means warm, solid, the real thing. Correct me if I'm wrong.

PENNY.   Fine, dad, fine. Just quit while you're ahead.

ARTHUR.   I won't say he was like a son to me. Even my son isn't always like a son to me. I mean...! In my clumsy way, I'm trying to say how much I like André. And how much he helped me to know my own boy. Cal was always two hands full but André and I could talk about anything under the sun. My wife was very fond of him, too.

PENNY.   Cal, I don't understand about the balloons.

CAL.   They represent the soul. When you let go, it means you're letting his soul ascend to heaven. That you're willing to let go. Breaking the last earthly ties.

PENNY.   Does the Pope know about this?

ARTHUR.   Penny!

PENNY.   André loved my sense of humor. Listen, you can hear him laughing. *(She lets go of her white balloon.)* So long, you glorious, wonderful. I-know-what-Cal-means-about-words ... *man!* God forgive me for wishing you were straight every time I laid eyes on you. But if any man was going to have you, I'm glad it was my brother! Look how fast it went up. I bet that means something. Something terrific. *(Arthur lets his balloon go.)*

ARTHUR.   Goodbye. God speed.

PENNY.   Cal?

CAL.   I'm not ready yet.

PENNY.   Okay. We'll be over there. Come on, pop, you can buy your little girl a Good Humor.

ARTHUR.   They still make Good Humor?

PENNY.   Only now they're called Dove Bars and they cost 12 dollars. *(Penny takes Arthur off. Cal and André's Mother stand with their balloons.)*

CAL.   I wish I knew what you were thinking. I think it would help me. You know almost nothing about me and I only know what André told me about you. I'd always had it in my mind that one day we would be friends, you and me. But if you didn't know about André and me.... If this hadn't happened, I wonder if he would have ever told you. When he was so sick, if I asked him once I asked him a thousand times, tell her. She's your mother. She won't mind. But he was so afraid of hurting you and of your disapproval. I don't know which was worse. *(No response. No sighs.)* God, how many of us live in this city because we don't want to hurt our mothers and live in mortal terror of their disapproval. We loose ourselves here. Our lives aren't furtive, just our feelings towards people like you are! A city of fugitives from our parents' scorn or heartbreak. Sometimes he'd seem a little down and I'd say, "What's the matter, babe!" And this funny sweet, sad smile would cross his face and he'd say, "Just a little homesick, Cal, just a little bit." I always accused him of being a country boy just playing at being a hot shot, sophisticated New Yorker. *(He sighs.)* It's bullshit. It's all bullshit. *(Still no response.)* Do you remember the comic strip *Little Lulu?* Her mother had no name, she was so remote, so formidable to all the children. She was just Lulu's mother. "Hello, Lulu's Mother," Lulu's friends would say. She was almost anonymous in her remoteness. You remind me of her. André's mother. Let me answer the questions you can't ask and then I'll leave you alone and you won't ever have to see me again. André died of AIDS. I don't know how he got it. I tested negative. He died bravely. You would have been proud of him. The only thing that frightened him was you. I'll have everything that was his sent to you. I'll pay for it. There isn't much. You should have come up the summer he played *Hamlet.* He was magnificent. Yes, I'm bitter. I'm bitter I've lost him. I'm bitter what's happening. I'm bitter even now, after all this, I can't reach you. I'm beginning to feel your disapproval and it's making me ill. *(He looks at his balloon.)* Sorry, old friend. I blew it. *(He lets go of the balloon.)* Good night, sweet prince, and flights of angels sing thee to thy rest! *(Beat.)* Goodbye, André's mother. *(He goes. André's Mother stands alone holding her white balloon. Her lip trembles. She looks on the verge of breaking down. She is about to let go of the balloon when she pulls it down to her. She looks at it a while before she gently kisses it. She lets go of the balloon. She follows it with her eyes as it rises and rises. The lights are beginning to fade. André's Mother's eyes are still on the balloon. Blackout.)*

THE END

PROPERTY LIST

4 helium-filled balloons